George Leavitt and Co.

Choice Paintings

George Leavitt and Co.

Choice Paintings

ISBN/EAN: 9783744622042

Printed in Europe, USA, Canada, Australia, Japan

Cover: Foto ©Thomas Meinert / pixelio.de

More available books at **www.hansebooks.com**

The
Spencer
Collection.

LEAVITT ART GALLERIES,

817 BROADWAY

CHOICE PAINTINGS.

THE PRIVATE COLLECTION

FORMED BY

MR. ALBERT SPENCER,

ON EXHIBITION, DAY AND EVENING,

AT THE

LEAVITT ART GALLERIES,

817 BROADWAY, COR. OF 12th STREET,

(From Wednesday, March 26th, until Thursday, April 3d.)

THE COLLECTION WILL BE SOLD

AT

CLINTON HALL,

Astor Place,

ON THE EVENING OF THURSDAY, APRIL 3D,

At Half-past Seven O'clock.

GEO. A. LEAVITT & CO., R. SOMERVILLE,
Auctioneers.

_ Sale under the Supervision of S. P. AVERY. *_*

ARTISTS REPRESENTED IN
THIS COLLECTION.

CRITICAL NOTICE

OF THE

COLLECTION.

THE collection here assembled is in the best sense an expression of the critical opinions and chastened tastes of a refined connoisseur. Every private gallery should be so, indeed ; but how many private galleries do we find to be merely the advertisement of a buyer's wealth or knowledge of artistic names—a display to be rattled before the eyes of society, much as the owner rattles the money in his pockets ! Here, on the contrary, every canvas has been weighed, estimated, carried up to a standard. Some collections are like the library of Mr. Potiphar, which contained the names of all the great authors pasted upon blocks of wood ; but others are like the working library of Joubert, who never would own a complete Rousseau or an unexpurgated Voltaire, and whose books were the books that assimilated with his thoughts and formed his character. This collection of paintings is of the latter order, and to have loved them all is what it was to have loved the Lady Elizabeth Hastings, in Steele's *Tattler* essay—"a liberal education."

Seldom in a picture gallery do we find such a choice average—an average expressed in such varieties of excellence. The painters who enjoyed the owner's predilection are represented in their whole octave, from their most minute and individual studies to their broadest effects. It is a chance to estimate the length and the breadth of the greatest modern talents. For instance, the late Narcisse Diaz is represented by five examples, showing him as the great figure-painter and colorist, as well as the sumptuous landscapist. Jacque is seen in four specimens, Schreyer in three large and important ones, the magical Boldini in five of his sunny caprices, Madrazo in four examples, of which one is a *morceau de roi*, Plassan in four, Van Marcke in three. In this liberal gallery we are allowed not merely to see the man of genius in a single aspect, but to walk all round him. There is nothing cumbrous, however, in this full representation. The specimens are of medium size, besides being in brilliant condition. It is a gent'eman's collection of favorites ; not a cicerone's exhibit of colossi. The owner has been a liberal patron of artists, and a discreet watcher of opportunities. Many of the examples were imported expressly to his order; others were purchased from such renowned collections as the Parisian one of W. H. STEWART, Esq.; or the American galleries of E. MATTHEWS, J. STRICKER JENKINS, Esquires, and others. That he has been a liberal buyer, our most intelligent importers of art, such as Messrs. Knoedler, Avery, Schaus, and Kohn, can testify.

It is hard to examine such a collection cursorily, for a hasty glance is apt to be prolonged to a minute scrutiny; but a quick bird's-eye view is all that this rapid summary can undertake.

The grand, serious interpreters of rustic Nature in Europe have been terribly thinned off by death of late. Millet, Diaz, Daubigny, Troyon, Fromentin, Corot, are no more. Yet they live still, in a manner, within the limits of a collection such as this, which guards untarnished the most vital emanations of their minds.

J. F. Millet, the hermit of the Fontainebleau forest, the poetic painter who associated with peasants, and wrung out the secret of their grimy lives, has never been approached for a peculiar massive nobility of treatment, appro-

priate to the rugged seriousness of the life he
interprets. His simplicity is pregnant with
matter, and his themes show all the melan-
choly grandeurs of poverty, like the verselets
of Gray's *Elegy*. See how seriously his "Barbizon Shepherdess" knits, in the example of
this gallery ! If she were a rural Fate, com-
plicating the thread of destiny for the obscure
lives around her, she could not be more ab-
sorbed and have a more introverted expression.
Her toil is an emblem of the peasant's narrow
cares, keeping the eye down steadily from the
horizon. Meanwhile, beyond the close thicket
where she waits in her wooden shoes, the sul-
len threshers are bending over the harvest, in
a gleam of unwilling and difficult sunshine.
A picture by Millet is Toil chanting its own
sad poetry.

Diaz is so well represented in this collection, that, in his case, the epitaph of Pope on
Newton might almost be reversed ; the genius
that the grave and the monument declare
mortal, these bursts of splendor declare im-
mortal. Watch these Persian children of his,
the offspring of his soul and his genius, as
they disport in an Oriental game akin to blindman's buff ! There are thirteen of them, and
they mix in the intricacies of their play like
a bouquet of gorgeous blossoms. What the
painter is seeking is not so much their grace ·

of posture or anatomical exactitude, as the opulence of their tints, their complexions gilded by the eastern sun, the contrast of cloth of gold flashing against brocade. It is flower-painting applied to humanity, with a primary importance accorded to color. Diaz, one of the Spanish refugees in France from the conquest of Spain by Napoleon, lived among the Parisian painters like an apostle of Color. He brought up with him the glowing traditions of Velasquez and Murillo, and opposed those rich, succulent theories of painting to the colder methods of Delaroche and Ingres. A charming companion among the more northerly comrades of his choice, yielding sometimes to his temptations to quick retorts and Castilian temper, he stumped about among them on his wooden leg, and died in their midst the other day, an imported patriarch whom everybody honored. If in his figure-groups he was especially a colorist, in his landscapes he was a *luminarist*. None could excel him in introducing a rain of silver light through the velvet closeness of a thick and tufted wood, overgrown with lichen, and dry with the hot evaporation of summer. One of his characteristic effects is seen here, where a theatre of trees closes in a circle around an open space within, and the sparse light crumbles its splintery rays against the mossy tree-trunks.

Another, of a rarer style for the artist, displays a free horizon and a broad plain—the "Plain of Barbizon." It is as successful in its broad escape as the other in its voluntary confinement, and the light basks solid and unconfined on the round lake in the centre. The five examples of Diaz, however, include the whole circumference of his talent, and form a better explanation of the man than any written commentary.

Daubigny, lost too early to art a short time since, was a twilight dreamer by river banks, a poet of grave and vibrating notes, inimitable for breadth and sweetness. The charm of his limpid rivers, his green banks set with shadowy cottage walls and sleeping under the evening star, has never been exceeded. The collection contains a characteristic example of his pensive, noble style.

Dupré, the colleague and contemporary of these great artists, still survives, perpetuating in a later day the masterly methods of a grand landscape *renaissance*. He came to the front along with Rousseau and Decamps and Troyon. He is unexcelled in the solid splendor of his sunshine, the knowledge of effect which secures luminousness. Couture, in his curious memoirs, gives Dupré his full importance, acknowledging the dazzling force of his *impasto*, and allying him with Decamps and the great masters of the Romantic revival. The two river scenes in this gallery display his solid, satisfying chiaroscuro and rich color.

Jacque, too, survives, the unrivaled master of light and shade, the Rembrandt-like etcher, the strong realist in landscape, the versatile sheep-painter, poultry-painter, and sketcher of cottage life. One of the smaller examples in the collection, entitled "Ploughing," displays him at his very highest flight ; it is greatly like a Millet ; the rich contrast of tones is full of grandeur and force, as the ploughman drives his horses through the dark shadow of a horizontal stretch of cloud, while the distance is washed with a pale and dying train of sunlight. A larger composition shows his familiar sheep, huddled under a group of gnarled and iron-limbed oaks, in all the solidity and bold relief of nature. In other examples, notably the "Mule-Driver's Luncheon," the practical, positive, learned handling of Jacque is variously exemplified.

Troyon, the great master of cattle-painting and landscape, the introducer of a style, the discoverer of the merits of Constable, the pioneer of realism and nature study in scenery, died with the honors of a precursor and the glory of an inventor. His works are sought as no other animalist's works of modern times are sought. Of his mighty talent, the admi-

1*

rable study of an ox, seen here in the midst of
a strong, dark landscape, is an example full of
the master's peculiar individuality.

His brilliant surviving pupil, Van Marcke,
is fast becoming his rival. What was impress-
ive in Troyon by way of breadth and massive-
ness, is seductive in Van Marcke from its
sunny glitter and surprise of contrasts. There
are three of his luminous, silken-skinned ani-
mal subjects represented.

With Schreyer (of Paris, notwithstanding
his German name), we leave the placid languor
of the herd, and come upon exciting dramas
and hair-breadth 'scapes. He has studied, as
no one else has, the forms and movements of
the furry, big-headed, indefatigable horses of
Hungary and Wallachia. The silken barb
of Algeria is equally the slave of his cunning
pencil. The specimens of Schreyer in this
collection are large, adequate, and important,
whether he gives us the exciting race of Rus-
sian travelers from famished wolves in eternal
snows, or the gorgeous pageantry of Oriental
equestrianism, or the gaunt, gipsy-like rugged-
ness of the Wallachian convoy.

Fromentin, another of the great names gone,
was a painter who loved the desert, not from
any wildness or misanthropy of character, but
because its poetical forms and colors appealed
to the decorative aptitudes of his nature, like

a fairy pantomime. He painted an East that
was all grace, harmony, and mellow beauty,
like the East of *Lalla Rookh*. In the present
example the Orient is not arid nor lonely, but
green with the deep verdure of an oasis, in
which repose a couple of horses, silken-skinned and graceful. Fromentin always painted
like the poet and man of culture he really
was.

His rival and equal survives him—Alberto
Pasini, born near Parma, but Parisian by adop-
tion. His works, based on the exactest sci-
ence, are a revelation of the joyous glitter and
magical sunshine of the East—confused at
first sight, but resolvable into the most exact
facts and details. In the glorious example
here seen, the piled domes of St. Sophia glitter in the sun, the swinging gilded chariot
gives issue to the Sultan's harem as they enter
the portal, and the grouped horses of the im-
perial guard melt into the warm light that
caresses everything. Pasini is here seen like
the magician of Aladdin's palace, instantly
building with jewels and precious metals a
window into the Orient.

Gérôme, one of the kings of modern painting, a many-sided intellect that has left hardly
a department of art untouched and unadorned
—Gérôme holds the Orient in fee, too, among
his various provinces. It is unnecessary to

dilate on the greatness of this painter of the
"Death of Cæsar" and "Pollice Verso."
Nowhere is his talent more sure and definite
than in his oriental scenes, where, as in this
"Master of the Hounds," the forms of a brace
of tawny African grey-hounds, or the type and
costume of a laughing native, are seized with
the inexorable realism of a photographer and
the accidental felicity of a Gavarni. This
picture, painted to order for our collector,
is a *résumé* of the chiseled perfection of
Gérôme.

His fellow - professor of the Beaux-Arts
school, Cabanel, is, with Couture, one of the
few artists who still cultivate ideal beauty and
poetic feminine grace in the age of realism
which enjoys the novels of Zola and the can-
vases of Manet. Cabanel is represented by an
"Ophelia," a most touching and divinely
beautiful life-size head, every way worthy of
the painter of the "Venus" and the "Floren-
tine Poet," and in whose physiognomy we
seem to see a glimpse of the greatest Ophelia
of the stage, Mlle. Nilsson.

Couture, the author of that mighty page
"The Decadence of the Romans," a grand
champion of idealism in art against the invading
forces of the "practicals," is represented in
character by a lovely example called "The
Return from the Fields." It is a life-size bust

picture, showing a boy bearing an armful of brilliant poppies.

Meissonier remains, after all, the standard of the art of painting as an art, the sum of technical skill and knowledge. None but he quite solves the problem of painting in the grand manner on a small scale. Measures and dimensions are an impertinence in estimating his work, which is equally grand whether seen through the large end or the small end of a lorgnette. His "Vedette," * in this collection, shows a flush of blue daylight and a statuesque figure in uniform, all on a large scale for the master, and his "Cavalier," a handsome squire of the Louis XIII. period, idly switching his whip as he waits beneath Marion Delorme's balcony, is one of his gem-like pieces of sculpture with the brush in color. Both are inimitable by any other painter.

* Upon the back of this picture is an original letter by the artist, of which this is a translation. "I thank Mr. ——, for his visit to Poissy, and I am so much the more flattered that he informs me that he has just purchased my ‘ Republican Sentinel of the Army of the Var.’ I take great pleasure in repeating to him what I said to my friend, Mr. Petit, who has ceded him this picture ; it is the first time that I sign a painting with which I am absolutely satisfied.

"E. MEISSONIER."

" Poissy, 29 August, 1875."

Jules Lefebvre is the acknowledged master of
the nude, treated in a chaste and classical temper that elevates the facts of anatomy into noble and ideal lessons. One of his very best
themes, though small, is the "Magdalen,"
seen here in her abject bareness of all relief
and comfort. The technical mastery of this
figure is only equaled by its classical purity
and elevation. Another painter, who is all
delicacy and poetry, is Jalabert, whose youth
was passed along with that of Gérôme and
Cabanel. His "Romeo and Juliet" is ten-
der, luscious and pathetic. The style of Jules
Breton is adequately indicated in his pupil,
Billet's, picture, of a reclining shepherdess.
Merle, one of the most popular painters living
for feminine and infantine subjects, is represented by a group as charming as a poem of
Longfellow's ; it is called "Once upon a
Time," and represents legendary lore in the
person of a grandame, entertaining six young-
sters with same sweet tale, the same breath
from long ago. Bouguereau, whose serene
and thoughtful religious themes have lately
been elevating him in European estimation to
a still higher rank than heretofore, is best
known in this country by his elegant child
subjects, of which a good specimen is this
thoughtful little maid, who grasps her violets
as who should grasp the hands of sisters, and

whose sweet youth exhales a perfume of the woodland and the flower bank.

Knaus, the grand chief of *genre* art, the greatest outcome of the familiar Düsseldorf character-painters, is represented by a sweet and thoughtful peasant girl's head. Carl Becker, one of the most brilliant living painters of rich stuffs and handsome, blonde faces, contributes a Venetian girl in a picturesque costume. In another style, Boughton, the painter whom America has regretfully lost to England, shows female loveliness treated in allegory, when he gives us, as "Morning," a richly-dight maiden dipping a bare foot into the spring. Willems, the inheritor of the exquisite art of Terburg, exults in his rendering of white satin in the fair subject of the lute-playing scene he paints so delicately. Toulmouche, one of the most finished painters of feminine coquetries, shows us a maid of eighteen, reclining on a sofa, like Mme. Recamier in David's picture, and with sofa, screen, pink dress, fan, and slippers all consistent with the supposed date of 1820 or thereabouts.

Another painter of *la femme*, Plassan, who is only not renowned as a grand colorist because he chooses to paint but in cabinet size, is represented in four works, showing the length and breadth of his rare, perfumed, flower-like talent. "The First-born" is a

home group in old Flemish costume, all but
the infant, who is not costumed at all ; the
turquoise blue of the proud mother's robe
is a revelation in color treatment. "Les
Femmes Savantes," with seven figures, is one
of his most important works. Among the
other contributions of this habitual devotee of
women, will be found a surprise, a landscape
of rare delicacy and sincerity.

This sudden and rather startling divergence
into landscape subjects may be the excuse for
referring here to some scenery in the collection that is out of the common, and individual
—such as Ciceri's river with pollard oaks
and groups of peasants, most real, intense,
and daylight-like ; and Clays', the great Bel-
gian master of river-scenery, showing Dutch
boats on limpid, idle water. Here, too, may
be mentioned such crisp bits of actuality as De
Neuville's " Franc-tireurs "—a couple of these
ac.ive sharpshooters receiving an indication of
the Prussians' whereabouts from a garde-cham-
pêtre in blue blouse ; and Detaille's " Out-
posts," a picket in the snow—both painted
with all the energy and exactitude of these con-
scientious drill-masters of military art. Vibert
is long famous as one of the greatest humorists
and most finished draughtsmen living : he has
seldom sent from the easel aught more telling
than this study of a young ecclesiastic in scar-

let, buried in the innumerable folio authorities collected for the composing of his first sermon.

Returning to the always delightful limners of feminine beauty, we perceive Aubert, the legitimate successor of Hamon, whose fairy-like transmuting talent turned whole generations of the last female decade to roses and butterflies. Aubert's contribution, in a similar vein of parable, shows "Love's Entanglement," a girl whose distaff has been seized by Cupid, and will turn out a thread not of her own weaving or intention. Jacquet, one of the most highly esteemed of younger artists, whose "Reverie" is a late prize of the Luxembourg collection, is represented by the profile of a beautiful and meditative blonde.

A wonderful confidant of the feminine nature is Comte-Calix; how he enters into the sentiment, the tenderness, or the playful mischief, of his soft-haired, romantic heroines! He contributes a peasant-girl of La Bresse (a town near Montargis), as seen "Going to Market." The face is sweet and lovely, to the very limit of peasant-probability, and the quaint head-dress does no harm to its provincial type of beauty. Apropos of this charming coiffure, hear Hamerton, one of the first of art critics; in his "Round my House" he narrates his mild shipwreck in a river-steamer,

and the detention of his fair fellow-passengers
who were going to market.

" Let us hope that the peasant women of La Bresse
got their apples and cheese to market. They were all
the more interesting for that funny, but not altogether
unbecoming, costume of theirs, with its especially re-
markable head-dress. It is like a stool wrong side
up, with its one leg in the air, the large round disc being flat on the head, with four curtains of black lace
hanging from it, two on each side, and a narrow va-
lence of the same material all around it. The rest of
the costume is quaint and picturesque, and has a
pretty coquettish look when it is new, with the short
petticoats, neat aprons, and broad bands of velvet on
the bodices."

A well-served *Diner à la Russe* will offer
you a sweet water-ice right in the middle, and
the most piquant flavor of game at the end.
Fearing lest even this summary article should
cloy the appetite with its feast of delicacies,
there has been carefully introduced in the
midst this bevy of beauties by Aubert, Jacquet and Comte-Calix, while a totally new
flavor, the flavor of the so called "Spanish-
Roman School," has been saved for the close.
The unspeakable, brilliant, gem-like pa-
lette of the late Fortuny did not sink into the
tomb without leaving inheritors. Bringing
into Rome, from his recollections of the Ve-
lasques, the Goyas, the Riberas of the Madrid

Gallery, a strangely lucid and positive way
of looking at nature, Fortuny introduced a
novel kind of study to the Romans. The
exact effects and reliefs of sunlight were to be
represented, without conventionality or de-
pendence on former interpreters. The dazzling ability of Fortuny has been in great
measure bequeathed to a band of artists, who
continue his line, such as Villegas, Boldini,
Madrazo, and Martin Rico. The present collector has been an enlightened encourager of
this unconventional and innovating form of
art ; and the gallery is largely tinctured with
it. The Boldinis, five in number, exult in
the frank noonday sunshine, which dissimulates
nothing, and overshadows no difficulties
slighted. In this study of a young lady in
the grass, with dog and parasol, and a line of
woods in the background, the very glint of sun
on sward and trees is obtained as by magic,
with its powder of dust and blue reflections.
The girl in Reine Hortense costume, who
reads her novel on a garden bench ; the " Parisiennes," one smoking cigarettes at the window, the other (in black silk) smoking them
over *Figaro* as she reposes ; the water-color of
a girl in *Directoire* dress, going in at a gloomy
door, which relieves her brilliant toilette ; the
" Matador and his Sweetheart," playing with
the cockatoo ; all of these are frank experi-

ments of painting *à la tache*, to get the exact values of nature and the inter-reflections of one color upon another. As realistic studies they are like a falling of scales from the eyes. As bits of character they are piquant as any comic opera.

The Madrazo's, of which there are four, show a broader, larger touch. If Boldini might be called the Detaille of the Spanish-Roman School, Madrazo might be named its Meissonier : everything is subordinate to breadth, even in the most minute work of Madrazo. His girl in a garden, in rose-colored silk, watching the butterflies, is in breadth and delicate largeness of style a counterpart of corresponding figures by Alfred Stevens. As for his large picture in the collection, it is one of his most serious efforts, and almost beyond praise. It represents ladies coming from a church door through files of beggars, while a seller of relics supplies them with rosaries, and the relic-seller's child plays unconcernedly. The relations of the figures to the architecture, the individual solidity of each, combined with generalized grouping, and the local color expressed in the whole scene and every typical face, all stamp this as a masterpiece. For another quality, for transparent, porcelain-like lucidity of style, no living painter surpasses Villegas ; his study in water-color of a

burly fellow with drawn sword, is rich with vi-
tality and pure limpid color. In landscape,
Rico's view of a stream and old houses, near
Chartres, recalls much of Fortuny's felicity,
with similar effec s of sunshine and glitter.

With apologies for having kept the reader so
long from the more satisfying inspection of the
works themselves, the introductory notice
here closes.

The seventy-one numbers include the en-
tire collection of Mr. Spencer, without reserva-
tion or addition. The illustrations * for this
catalogue were drawn from the paintings by
Mr. Jas. D. Smillie, and reproduced by the
Photo-Engraving Co. The sale is made under
the direction of S. P. Avery, 86 Fifth Avenue.

* (The intention was to have many more engrav-
ings, but there was not sufficient time, consequently
some of the best works in the collection are not thus
represented.)

CATALOGUE.

SPENCER COLLECTION.

Sale on Thursday Evening, April 3.

(The first figure of the measure is the width.)

---

1. BROWN (JOHN LEWIS),   Paris
Medals, 1865, '66, '67.
Legion of Honor, 1870.
FORDING THE STREAM.
7 x 5

J. T. Johnston

12'.

2. BRILLOUIN (L. G.),   Paris
Pupil of Drolling.
Medals, 1865, '69, '74.
THE READER.
5 x 7

1, 0,

3. VILLEGAS,   Rome
A BULL FIGHTER.
Water-Color.
8 x 11

14, 0.

4. JACQUE (CHARLES),   Paris
Medals, 1861, '63, '64.
Legion of Honor, 1867.
A BARN-YARD.
16 x 21

2'.

9 6

238. Mad. Ave

5. VIBERT (J. G.),

Pupil of Barrias.

Medals, 1864, '67, '68.

Legion of Honor, 1870.

Medal at Exposition Universal, 1878.

AFTER DESSERT.

Water-Color.

14 x 10

6. VAN MARCKE (E.),

Pupil of Troyon.

Medals, 1867, '69, '74.

Legion of Honor, 1872.

Medal at Exposition Universal, 1878.

CATTLE.

13 x 9

7. PLASSAN (A. E.),

Medals, 1852, '57, '59.

Legion of Honor, 1859.

ON THE SEINE.

8 x 4

8. BILLET (PIERRE),

Pupil of Jules Breton.

Medals, 1873, '74.

A YOUNG SHEPHERDESS.

17 x 13

25

9. MADRAZO (RAIMOND DE),   Paris
Pupil of his Father.
Legion of Honor, 1878.
Medal at Exposition Universal, 1878.
LA SIGNORITA.
4 x 6

10. DÉTAILLE (E.),   Paris
Pupil of Meissonier.
Medals, 1869, '70, '72.
Legion of Honor, 1873.
THE OUTPOST.
Water-Color.
6½ x 9½

11. DIAZ (N.), Dec'd.   Paris
Medals, 1844, '46, '48.
Legion of Honor, 1851.
Diploma to the memory of deceased artists,
Exposition Universal, 1878.
LANDSCAPE.
13 x 9

12. BOLDINI (G.),   Paris
LADY OF THE EMPIRE.
Water-Color.
13 x 9

13. TROYON (CONSTANT), Dec'd.   Paris
Pupil of Rivereux.
Medals, 1838, '40, '46, '48, '55.
Legion of Honor, 1849.
A STUDY.
12 x 9

2

600

14. FALERO (RICARDO),   **Paris**

EASTERN DANCING WOMAN.

7 x 10

G. P. Huntington
6 r. Park ave

15. DUPRÉ (JULES),   **Paris**

Medals, 1833, (E. U.) '67.

Legion of Honor, 1849.

Officer of the Legion of Honor, 1870.

LANDSCAPE.

12 x 8

4 7/2

C. A. Turner

16. JACQUE (CHARLES),   **Paris**

Medals, 1861, '63, '64.

Legion of Honor, 1867.

LUNCH TIME.

8 x 11

G. G. Haven

17. JACQUET (J. G.),   **Paris**

Pupil of Bouguereau.

Medals, 1868, '75.

Medal at Exposition Universal, 1878.

FEMALE HEAD.

9 x 12

4 v 0.

C. K. King
180 5th Ave

18. PLASSAN (A. E.),   **Paris**

Medals, 1852, '57, '59.

Legion of Honor, 1859.

THE FIRST-BORN.

9 x 12

4 7/2

M. K. Jesup
197. mad. ave.

19. ZAMACOIS (EDOUARD), Dec'd.   Paris

Pupil of Meissonier.
Medal, 1867.
Diploma to the memory of deceased artists, Exposition Universal, 1878.

MEDITATION.

3 x 5

20. DESGOFFE (BLAISE),   Paris

Pupil of Flandrin.
Medals, 1861, '63.
Legion of Honor, 1878.
Honorable mention, Exposition Universal, 1878.

OBJECTS OF ART.

9 x 5

21. CICÉRI (E.),   Paris

Pupil of his Father.
Medal, 1852.
LANDSCAPE.
21 x 23

22. BECKER (CARL),   Berlin

Medal, 1861.
VENETIAN GIRL.
18 x 24

23. BELLECOUR (BERNE),   Paris

Pupil of Picot.
Medals, 1869, '72.
Medal at Exposition Universal, 1878.

THE PARROT.
Water-Color.
14 x 20

24. DIAZ (N.), Dec'd. **Paris**

Medals, 1844, '46, '48.
Legion of Honor, 1851.
Diploma to the memory of deceased artists, Exposition Universal, 1878.
ON THE EDGE OF THE FOREST.
14 x 10

25. TOULMOUCHE (A.), **Paris**

Pupil of Gleyre.
Medals, 1852, '59, '61.
Legion of Honor, 1870.
Medal at Exposition Universal, 1878.
FRENCH BOUDOIR.
9 x 12

26. BOLDINI (G.), **Paris**

THE GARDEN SEAT. EMPIRE.
5 x 7

27. COMPTE-CALIX (F. C.), **Paris**

Pupil of the Beaux-Art School, Lyons.
Medals, 1844, '57, '59, '63.
GOING TO MARKET.
15 x 21

28. AUBERT (JEAN), **Paris**

Pupil of P. Delaroche.
Prize of Rome, 1844.
Medals, 1857, '59, '61, '78.
LOVE'S ENTANGLEMENTS.
16 x 20

29. JACQUE (CHARLES),   Paris

Medals, 1861, '63, '64.

Legion of Honor, 1867.

PLOUGHING, SPRING-TIME.

18 x 9

30. SCHREYER (AD.),   Paris

Medals, 1864, '65, '67. (E. U.)

Vienna Exposition, 1873.

A BULGARIAN TRAIN.

32 x 18

31. DAUBIGNY (C. F.), Dec'd.   Paris

Pupil of C. Delaroche.

Medals, 1848, '53, '55, '57, '59, '67. (E. U.)

Legion of Honor, 1859.

Officer of the Legion of Honor, 1874.

Diploma to the Memory of deceased artists,

Exposition Universal, 1878.

RIVER LANDSCAPE.

22 x 14

32. GOUBIE (J. R.),   Paris

Pupil of Gérôme.

Medal, 1874.

ASKING THE WAY.

19 x 14

33. ESCOSURA (LEON),   Paris

Pupil of Gérôme.

Commander of the Order of Isabel the Catholic.

Chevalier of the Order of Charles III. of Spain.

Chevalier of the Order of Christ, of Portugal.

A GAME OF CHESS.

11 x 15

2*

34. RICO (M. D.),　　　　　　　　　　　　**Paris**

Pupil of Madrazo.

Medal at Exposition Universal, 1878.

NEAR CHARTRES.

7 x 11

35. WILLEMS (F.),　　　　　　　　　　　**Paris**

Medal, 1844, '46, '55, '67. (E. U.)

Medal at Brussels, 1843.

Chevalier of the Order of Leopold.

Legion of Honor, 1853.

Officer of the Order of Leopold, 1855.

Officer of the Legion of Honor, 1864.

Medal at Exposition Universal, 1878.

THE GUITAR.

10 x 12

36. CLAYS (P. J.),　　　　　　　　　　**Brussels**

Medal, 1867. (E. U.)

Legion of Honor, 1875.

Chevalier of the Order of Leopold.

Medal at Exposition Universal, 1878.

OFF THE COAST OF HOLLAND.

22 x 15

37. LeFEBVRE (JULES),　　　　　　　　**Paris**

Pupil of Cogniet.

Prize of Rome, 1861.

Medals, 1861, '65, '68, '70.

Legion of Honor, 1870.

Officer of the Legion of Honor, 1878.

Medal at Exposition Universal, 1878.

MAGDALEN.

11 x 7

38. DeNEUVILLE (A.), Paris

Pupil of Picot.

Medals, 1859, '61.

Legion of Honor, 1873.

FRENCH SHARP-SHOOTERS, 1871.

25 x 19

39. JACQUE (CHARLES), Paris

Medals, 1861, '63, '64.

Legion of Honor, 1867.

LANDSCAPE AND SHEEP.

25 x 31

40. VAN THOREN (OTTO). Paris

Medal, 1865.

THE COMING STORM.

39 x 27

41. SCHREYER (AD.), Paris

Medals, 1864, '65, (E. U.) '67.

Vienna Exposition, 1873.

WINTER TRAVEL. RUSSIA.

54 x 34

42. CABANEL (A.),   **Paris**
Pupil of Picot.
Medals, 1852, (E. U.) '55.
Prize of Rome, 1845.
Legion of Honor, 1855.
Member of the Institute of France, 1863.
Officer of the Legion of Honor, 1864.
Grand Medal of Honor, 1865 and (E. U.) 1867.
Commander of the Legion of Honor, 1878.
Grand Medal of Honor (E. U.)
Professor in the School of the Beaux Arts.
OPHELIA.
23 x 27

43. PLASSAN (A. E.),   **Paris**
Medals, 1852, '57. '59.
Legion of Honor, 1859.
GATHERED FLOWERS.
19 x 25

44. MERLE (HUGHES),   **Paris**
Pupil of Cogniet.
Medals, 1861, '63.
Legion of Honor, 1866.
"ONCE UPON A TIME."
18 x 22

45. COUTURE (T.),   **Paris**
Pupil of Gros.
Medals, 1844. '47. '55.
Legion of Honor, 1848.
COMING FROM THE FIELDS.
21 x 25

46. BOUGHTON (GEO. H.), London
MORNING.
15 x 27

47. VIBERT (J. G.), Paris
Pupil of Barrias.
Medals, 1864, '67, '68.
Legion of Honor, 1870.
Medal at Exposition Universal, 1878.
COMPOSING A SERMON.
16 x 26

48. BOUGUEREAU (W. A.), Paris
Pupil of Picot.
Prize of Rome, 1850.
Medals, 1855, (E. U.) 1857, '67 (E. U.)
Legion of Honor, 1859.
Member of the Institute of France, 1876.
Officer of the Legion of Honor, 1876.
Medal of Honor, Exposition Universal, 1878.
THE VIOLET.
15 x 19

49. COROT (J. B. C), Dec'd. Paris
Pupil of V. Bertin.
Medals 1838, '48, '55, '67 (E. U.)
Legion of Honor, 1846.
Officer of the Legion of Honor, 1867.
Diploma to the memory of deceased artists,
Exposition Universal, 1878.
LANDSCAPE.
20 x 14

50. MADRAZO (RAIMOND DE),   **Paris**

Pupil of his Father.

Legion of Honor, 1878.

Medal at Exposition Universal, 1878.

THE BUTTERFLIES.

14 x 16

51. BOLDINI (G.),   **Paris**

LES PARISIENNES.

9 x 12

52. VAN MARCKE (E.),   **Paris**

Pupil of Troyon.

Medals, 1867, '69, '70.

Legion of Honor, 1872.

Medal at Exposition Universal, 1878.

COWS IN A POOL.

16 x 10

53. FROMENTIN (E.), Dec'd.   **Paris**

Pupil of Cabat.

Medals 1849, '57. '59, (E. U.) 1867.

Legion of Honor, 1859.

Officer in the Legion of Honor, 1869.

Diploma to the memory of deceased artists,

Exposition Universal, 1878.

SCENE IN THE ORIENT.

10 x 13

54. MEISSONIER (J. L. E.),   Paris
Pupil of Cogniet.
Medals, 1840, '41, '43, '48.
Legion of Honor, 1846.
Grand Medal of Honor, (E. U.) 1855.
Officer of the Legion of Honor, 1856.
Member of the Institute of France, 1861.
Honorary Member of the R. A., London.
One of the Eight Grand Medals of Honor, (E. U.)
1867.
Commander of the Legion of Honor, 1867.
Grand Medal of Honor, (E. U.) 1878.
CAVALIER, TIME LOUIS XIII.
Water-Color.
8 x 13

55. DUPRÉ (JULES),   Paris
Medals, 1833, (E. U.) '67.
Legion of Honor, 1849.
Officer of the Legion of Honor, 1870.
MORNING.
11 x 7

56. DIAZ (N.), Dec'd.   Paris
Medals, 1844, '46, '48.
Legion of Honor, 1851.
Diploma to the memory of deceased artists,
Exposition Universal, 1878.
PLAINS OF BARBIZON.
18 x 15

36

57. MILLET (J. F.), Dec'd.   **Paris**
Pupil of P. Delaroche.
Medals, 1853, '64, (E. U.) 1867.
Legion of Honor, 1868.
Diploma to the memory of deceased artists, Exposi-
tion Universal, 1878.
SHEPHERDESS OF BARBIZON.
10 x 14

58. BOLDINI (G.),   **Paris**
IN THE GRASS.
9 x 6

59 MADRAZO (RAIMOND DE),   **Paris**
Pupil of his Father.
Legion of Honor, 1878.
Medal at Exposition Universal, 1878.
SPANISH LADY PLAYING GUITAR.
4 x 6

60. KNAUS (L.),   **Berlin**
Pupil of the Dusseldorf Academy.
Medals, 1853, '55, (E. U.) 1857, '59.
Legion of Honor, 1859.
Grand Medal of Honor, (E. U.) 1867.
Officer of the Legion of Honor, 1867.
Professor in the Academy, Berlin.
FEMALE HEAD.
6 x 8

37

61. BOLDINI (G.),　　　　　Paris
A MATADOR AND HIS SWEETHEART.
13 x 9

62. GÉRÔME (J. L.),　　　　Paris
　Pupil of P. Delaroche.
　Medals, 1847, '48, '55 (E. U.)
　Legion of Honor, 1855.
Member of the Institute of France, 1865.
Honorary Member of R. A., London.
One of the Eight Grand Medals of Honor, (E. U.)
1867.
Officer of the Legion of Honor, 1867.
Grand Medal of Honor, 1874.
Commander of the Legion of Honor, 1878.
Medal, Sculpture, (E. U.) 1878.
Grand Medal of Honor, (E. U.) 1878.
Professor in the School of the Beaux Arts.
KEEPER OF THE HOUNDS.
15 x 21

63. VAN MARCKE (E.),　　　　Paris
　Pupil of Troyon.
　Medals, 1867, '69, '70.
　Legion of Honor, 1872.
Medal at Exposition Universal, 1878.
CATTLE IN A MEADOW.
20 x 14

1000. **64. JALABERT (C. F.),** **Paris**

Pupil of P. Delaroche.

Hm Goddard Medals, 1847, '51, '53, '55, (E. U.) '67 (E. U.)

Legion of Honor, 1855.

Providence Officer of the Legion of Honor, 1867.

ROMEO AND JULIET.

15 x 19

2200 **65. DIAZ (N.), Dec'd.** **Paris**

Medals, 1844, '46, '48.

Legion of Honor, 1851.

1118. Cutting Diploma to the memory of deceased artists, Exposition

23. E. 24. Universal, 1878.

FOREST OF FONTAINEBLEAU.

22 x 17

2100. **66. SCHREYER (AD.),** **Paris**

Medals, 1864, '65, (E. U.) '67.

L. G. Haven Vienna Exposition, 1873.

ARABS RESTING.

30 x 17

5300. **67. MADRAZO (RAIMOND DE),** **Paris**

Pupil of his Father.

First-Class Medal and Legion of Honor, Exposition

3. P. Zutler Universal, 1878.

ENTRANCE TO A SPANISH CHURCH.

39 x 25

73,15.

...

68. PASINI (A.),   Italy *2500.*

Pupil of Ciceri.

Medals, 1859, '63, '64.

Legion of Honor, 1868.

Medal at Vienna, 1873.

Chevalier of the Orders of St. Maurice and Lazare.

Officer of the Orders of Turkey and Persia.

Honorary Professor at the Academies of Parma and Turin.

Grand Medal of Honor, Exposition Universal, 1878.

MOSQUE OF ST. SOFIA.

26 x 36

69. MEISSONIER (J. L. E.),   Paris *2100.*

Pupil of Cogniet.

Medals, 1840, '41, '43, '48.

Legion of Honor, 1846.

Grand Medal of Honor, (E. U.) 1855.

Officer of the Legion of Honor, 1856.

Member of the Institute of France, 1861.

Honorary Member of the R. A., London.

One of the Eight Grand Medals of Honor, (E. U.) 1867.

Commander of the Legion of Honor, 1867.

Grand Medal of Honor, (E. U.) 1878.

A REPUBLICAN SENTINEL.

15 x 19

70. PLASSAN (A. E.),   **Paris**

Medals, 1852, '57, '59.

Legion of Honor, 1859.

"LA FEMME SAVANT."

28 x 14

71. DIAZ (N.), Dec'd.   **Paris**

Medals, 1844, '46, '48.

Legion of Honor, 1851.

Diploma to the memory of deceased artists, Exposition Universal, 1878.

BLINDMAN'S-BUFF.

18 x 14

Illustrated Catalogue.

A Catalogue of this Collection, with
24 illustrations, will be issued and for
Sale at the ART GALLERIES, 817
Broadway.